Pocahontas

by Carl W. Grody

HOUGHTON MIFFLIN   BOSTON

Jamestown settlement, 1622

Truth or Fiction?

Many people think they know the story of Pocahontas. It is often told this way:

Pocahontas was a Native American princess in the early 1600s. She lived near the English colony of Jamestown, Virginia. Pocahontas met a settler named Captain John Smith. She fell in love with him.

Pocahontas's father was the chief, Powhatan. He decided to have John Smith killed. Pocahontas jumped in the way. She talked her father out of killing Smith. Pocahontas and Smith lived happily ever after.

How much of this story is true? History is not clear.

Pocahontas saving John Smith's life, from a painting by John Gadsby Chapman

Pocahontas, or Matoaka

John Smith was the only person who ever said Pocahontas saved him. And nobody else ever said they saw it happen. Smith may have made the story up. If so, he was the first in a long line of storytellers who have repeated the legend.

But Pocahontas did save Jamestown. In fact, she has been called "The Mother of our Country."

Chief Powhatan (1547–1618)

A Girl Named Matoaka

Pocahontas was born around 1595. She may have had a hundred brothers and sisters. Her father, Chief Powhatan, had about a hundred wives. Pocahontas was his favorite child.

Pocahontas was a nickname that meant "playful one." Her real name was Matoaka.

Colonists arrive at Jamestown, Virginia, 1607.

In 1607, England sent 104 men and boys to build the colony of Jamestown. Pocahontas was about twelve years old. Few of the settlers were used to working in the wilderness. Most did not even know how to farm. They would have starved without help from the Powhatan Indians.

Pocahontas was very interested in the English settlers. She wanted to learn all about them. She brought them food and showed them how to grow corn.

Friend and Prisoner

John Smith was in charge of Jamestown. When friendship cooled between the settlers and Powhatan, Pocahontas remained a good friend of the colony. She warned Smith whenever her father was angry.

Smith left Jamestown in 1609 after injuring his leg. He went back to England to see a doctor. In Jamestown, the English told Pocahontas that Smith was dead.

Captain John Smith, c. 1616

Replica of three English ships to arrive in Jamestown

Pocahontas moved away from Jamestown. It is said that she married another Powhatan Indian. But an English captain found her in 1613. He invited her aboard his ship. Then he would not let her leave.

The English held Pocahontas for ransom. They wanted Powhatan to trade English prisoners for her. But Powhatan paid only part of the ransom, and Pocahontas stayed a prisoner.

Pocahontas marries John Rolfe

Rebecca Rolfe

Pocahontas was moved to a new settlement. A minister taught her about the Christian religion. Her name was changed to Rebecca. A year later she spoke with her brothers. She told them the English had treated her well and that she was in love with an English tobacco farmer. His name was John Rolfe.

Pocahontas married John Rolfe in 1614. They had a son named Thomas the next year.

Jamestown settlement, 1600s

Jamestown still struggled. English people were afraid to move to Virginia. But there was peace in Virginia after Pocahontas got married. Her marriage was seen as proof that the settlers could get along with the Native Americans.

In 1616, Pocahontas went to England with her husband and son. The English colonists wanted to show her off to English people. They wanted to prove that Native Americans were peaceful.

Pocahontas, dressed for her visit with royalty

Pocahontas in England

Pocahontas met the king and queen of England. She met the English public. She was a walking advertisement for the American colonies.

She also met John Smith again. She was shocked to see him. She had thought he was dead. But their meeting was not happy. They argued and never saw each other again.

Gravesend, England

Pocahontas stayed in England for seven months. In 1617, Rolfe was ready to go home. The family boarded a ship bound for Virginia. But the trip was short. Pocahontas had caught an illness. The ship went back to England. Pocahontas was taken to a town called Gravesend.

The Death of Pocahontas

Pocahontas comforted her husband and told him that it was enough that their child lived. She died and was buried in a Gravesend churchyard as Rebecca Rolfe. She was 22 years old.

John Rolfe went back to Virginia. He decided to leave their son Thomas in England. Thomas went to school there. He returned to Virginia as an adult.

Pocahontas and her son, Thomas

Colonists fighting Indians in Virginia, c. 1676

John Rolfe continued to grow tobacco in Virginia. The colony of Virginia began to grow. More English settlers arrived.

Unfortunately, the peace between the Indians and English settlers did not last long after the death of Pocahontas. Rolfe died in 1622, possibly in a battle with the Powhatans.

Title page from John Smith's book

"The Mother of Our Country"

John Smith wrote his story about Pocahontas in 1624. He described how she had saved his life. He never said that she loved him.

But storytellers thought that made a good reason why she saved him. A novelist named John Davis wrote a book about Pocahontas and John Smith in the 1790s. He wrote that they were in love.

Pocahontas statue in Jamestown, Virginia

No one will ever know what really happened. But there is no doubt that Pocahontas kept the settlers from starving to death. She stopped the war with the Native Americans long enough for Jamestown to grow. Her visit to England convinced more settlers to come to Jamestown.

Without Pocahontas, Jamestown may not have survived.